KT-102-698

PARROTS

IN this book, Mr. Rogers explains, simply and concisely, how Parrot-like birds should be managed so as to keep them in perfect health and feather and the treatment they need to make them gentle, playful and good talkers.

There is also first-class advice on exhibiting.

By the same author

BUDGERIGARS

CANARIES

PARROTS

BY

C. H. ROGERS F.B.S.A.

FOYLES HANDBOOKS
LONDON

© *W. & G. Foyle Ltd. 1958*

First published 1953
Reprinted 1958
Reprinted 1965
Reprinted 1967
Reprinted 1969
Reprinted 1971
Revised edition 1975
Reprinted 1977
Reprinted 1979
Reprinted 1984

ISBN 0 7071 0531 5

Published in Great Britain by
W. & G. Foyle Ltd
125 Charing Cross Road
London WC2H 0EB

Printed and bound in Great Britain
at The Pitman Press, Bath

CONTENTS

INTRODUCTION

THE large family of Parrot-like birds which are to be found wild over a very large area of the world are in all probability the oldest type of caged bird. Records of Parrot species are to be found in the old writings of the ancient Egyptians, Chinese and the Incas of South America. Parrot-like birds have a special attraction to both old and young alike, undoubtedly because of their beautiful colourings, amusing antics and wonderful powers of imitating the human voice. In this handbook I have endeavoured to explain simply and concisely how Parrot-like birds should be managed to keep them in perfect health and feather, and the treatment they need to make them gentle, playful and good talkers. Although there are many different breeds of Parrot-like birds ranging from the gigantic Macaws to the minute Pigmy Parrots they all require a similar sympathetic treatment. I feel sure that for anyone looking for a pet that is unusual and amusing, a Parrot is ideal, and it is hoped that this handbook will be helpful in the matter of selecting the right kind of Parrot.

CYRIL H. ROGERS.

CHAPTER 1

HISTORY

1. ANCIENT CAGE BIRDS

IT has become quite clear after studying the history of the early civilizations in the warmer parts of the globe, that Parrot-like birds were kept in captivity both as household pets and in decorated aviary structures. When the first members of the Parrot species actually came to this country it is difficult to ascertain, but undoubtedly odd specimens were brought over by the early traders from the near East. It is known that Alexander the Great brought tame Parrots from India to Rome where they became great favourites with the nobles of that time. The Romans housed their Parrots in cages made of ivory and precious metals and in most elaborate aviaries. Until the early part of this present century Parrots were mostly associated with sea-faring men and elderly ladies, although a few were kept by aviculturists, but now their cult is widespread and embraces people in all walks of life. The advent of the long distance sailing ships brought seamen into contact with countries where Parrots were amongst the wild birds and were kept as pets by the natives of those lands. Brightly coloured, strange-looking birds that could imitate the human voice must have appeared very fascinating to those adventurous seamen and it is little wonder that numerous specimens of the various kinds were brought back to this country as gifts for their families. Some of the earliest specimens of birds from foreign countries to be housed at the Zoological Gardens, London, were birds of the Parrot-like species. At the present time the Zoo has a wonderful and varied collection of Parrots, Macaws, Cockatoos, Parrakeets, etc., and the Parrot house is always a centre of attraction for visitors of all ages.

2. BAN ON IMPORTATIONS

Up to 1931, when a ban on the importation into this country of all Parrot-like birds was imposed, vast numbers of Parrots of all species came into this country often under very crowded conditions and the mortality was often high. The fact that Parrots were so easy to obtain did little to encourage aviculturists to attempt to breed them in this country. However, the application of the Parrot ban altered this outlook and quite a lot of Parrots, Parrakeets, etc., hitherto not bred in this country were reared by keen breeders. Because of the difficulty of breeding Parrot-like birds, and the fact that they could only be imported under special Government licence, made their value rise sharply and good talking birds or rare specimens could cost up to £100 each. In 1952 the Parrot ban was removed and once again Parrot-like birds have become more plentiful and consequently more reasonable in price. The ban was again imposed in the early part of 1953 and Parrot-like birds can only be imported under licence which should be applied for from the Ministry of Health, London. However, during the clear period, the stocks of Parrot-like birds in this country were replenished both as breeding birds and as pets. Air travel has made the importation of all kinds of birds so much more simple, and journeys which at one time took weeks can now be completed in a matter of hours. This quick method of travel allows birds to arrive in this country with little or no inconvenience and in a much better condition, consequently they are easier to acclimatize. The care and treatment of newly imported specimens are, as will be seen in Chapter 5, of utmost importance and actually control the length of the bird's life. Certain species of Parrot-like birds can live to a great age under favourable conditions and there are records showing they have survived over 100 years in captivity.

3. HABITAT

Parrots do not occur as wild birds (escaped specimens excepted) on the Continent of Europe proper and their distribution lies mainly within the tropical and sub-tropical areas of the world. There are many groups of related birds all having the distinct articulated upper mandible and paired toes which together form the extensive family of Parrot-like birds. In the next Chapter each of these groups has been dealt with separately and a description given of the more popular varieties. It will be realized that in a small handbook like this, it is not possible to give a fully detailed account of all the many forms. Should the reader require further and complete descriptive information it can be obtained from the many excellent specialized bird books of individual countries. Practically all members of the Parrot-like groups can be taught to talk, but their proficiency varies with the different varieties and also with individual specimens. Some of the species such as the African Greys and the Amazons have tremendous powers of reproduction of the human voice and other sounds, whilst further kinds do not talk so fluently, but become exceedingly tame and friendly and can be taught to do various tricks.

4. COLOUR VARIETIES

Many of the Parrakeets and Love Birds breed quite freely in captivity and with some of the species, colour varieties have been raised and perpetuated. The principal new coloured breeds are the Lutino Ring-necks (yellow birds with red eyes), Yellow Redrumps and Blue Love Birds, all of which are most attractive forms. Other species of Parrots and Cockatoos have been bred occasionally, and in another Chapter the breeding of Parrot-like birds in this country will be dealt with in a practical manner.

CHAPTER 2

VARIETIES

5. THE DIFFERENT TYPES

THE large family of Parrot-like birds can be divided into a number of different groups and representatives of all of them are kept here in Great Britain either as single pets or in collectors' aviaries. First come the typical Parrots, then the Macaws, Cockatoos, Conures, Love Birds, Pigmy Parrots, Parrakeets, Lorikeets and Lories. In the following paragraphs a description is given of the popular and most interesting members of each group commencing with the typical Parrots.

6. THE AFRICAN GREY PARROTS (*Psittacus erithacus*) (Fig. 1)

There can be little doubt that these Parrots are the most sought after and most popular of all the vast number of Parrots. They are invariably of gentle nature, easy to handle, require a simple diet, have a long life and a capacity for imitating the human voice with great accuracy. The Grey Parrots are about 13 ins. in length with a dark-coloured, stout hooked bill and bare patches of white skin surrounding the eyes; their size varies somewhat, with the females generally a little smaller. The body colour is a shaded dove grey with a short vivid red tail and under covets. These and other African Parrots require special care when first imported, but once they have become acclimatized they are, if properly managed, practically trouble-free. Correct feeding plays an important part in keeping all birds in perfect health and in good hard plumage. A sound staple seed mixture should consist of about 50 per cent large canary seed (Spanish canary type) and the remainder made up with equal parts of mixed sunflower seeds, safflower seeds, hemp, dari and a few whole oats and ground nuts. The actual percentages of the ingredients can be varied a little to suit the tastes of individual birds, but it is important that canary seed is always present in a good proportion. Chapter 4 deals fully with the feeding of all Parrot-like birds when they first arrive in this country and also when

Fig. I. AFRICAN GREY PARROT

they have become acclimatized. As a general rule African Greys are most friendly and gentle birds and are quite safe with children and animals. Although they have powerful beaks which can crack nuts with ease they will only attempt to bite if frightened, teased or ill-treated in any way. Birds which have spiteful habits have invariably been badly trained and roughly treated when first caught, but with kindness they can usually be cured. Greys have been known to form strong attachments to dogs, cats, monkeys and other birds and a great many stories are told as to their various exploits. Once the confidence of the birds has been gained, the owners can do practically anything with them and with care and patience they can be taught to perform most amusing tricks.

7. TIMNEH GREY PARROTS (*Psittacus Timneh*)
These attractive Parrots are very close relatives to the birds described in para. 6, but are only imported occasionally because

they are not so frequently taken by the native trappers. They are about 12 ins. in length which is slightly smaller than the common Greys and they are much darker in body colour throughout, with the tail and under covets being a dull reddish chocolate shade. Owners of Timneh Parrots all speak of their intelligence, gentleness and great powers of imitation. The general treatment, housing and feeding are the same as with the ordinary African Grey Parrots.

8. BROWN-HEADED PARROTS (*Poicephalus fuscicapillus*)

Another attractive type of African Parrot which has more variation in plumage than the Grey Parrots are the Brown-headed Parrots which are similar in size to that of the common Greys. Their head and neck feathers are silvery grey with rich brown centres and their foreheads a rosy red. The wing areas are a greenish brown shade and the butts of the wings and thighs are a red shade similar to that carried on the foreheads. Individual birds have been known to become very proficient talkers, but generally they are more reluctant to imitate than the Greys. However, what they lack in verbosity they make up for in tameness and brighter colouring of plumage.

9. SENEGAL PARROTS (*Poicephalus senegalus*) (Fig. 2)

Next to the Greys the charming friendly little Senegal Parrots are the most widely kept of all the many African Parrots. They are quite small birds between 9 ins. and 9½ ins. in length with dark grey heads and necks with lighter shading on the cheek patches. The upper part of the chest is green and the lower, in contrast, a bright orange yellow making a pleasing combination. Some birds show an extra amount of yellow in their plumage and it is thought that with a little careful breeding in captivity all yellow ones could be produced. Senegals are one of the easiest Parrots to train to perform tricks and are exceedingly gentle with their owners. Their powers to imitate seem to be somewhat limited although their enunciation is very clear and distinct. As with all kinds of Parrot-like birds, individuals of out-standing talking ability are met with occasionally. On account of their comparatively small size they are frequently kept in pairs in a normal-sized parrot cage. Senegals are equally gentle with their own species as they are with human beings. The antics of a pair

Fig. 2. SENEGAL PARROT

of Senegals either in a cage or breeding aviary can be a constant source of delight and amusement to their owners. They are extremely hardy birds and once acclimatized will live a great many years without the least trouble in their health.

10. MYER'S PARROTS *(Poicephalus meyeri)*
   These interesting Parrots are only imported into this country in spasmodic consignments and generally their distribution is inclined to be somewhat localised. If the opportunity to purchase should ever arise it should be taken, either for a household pet or to add to a collection of Parrot-like birds. They are only small birds being round about 9 ins. in length and their primary colouring is brown, green and yellow. With care they quickly become very tame and some are quite talkative to their owners, but rather shy with strangers.

11. OTHER MEMBERS OF THE POICEPHALUS SPECIES
   The following African Parrots are sometimes met in this

country, but the numbers imported are usually limited. BROWN-NECKED PARROTS (*P. rotustus*) head and neck grey-shaded with brown, body and rump green, wings dark green with thighs and wing butts vermillion red, overall length 13 ins., male and female similar in size. CONGO RED-HEADED PARROTS (*P. guilielmi*) top of head scarlet orange, body neck and wings green, thighs and wing butts same colour as head, overall length 11 ins. Near relatives to these Parrots are the *P. subryanus* which are a little larger in size and carry more red in their plumage. RED-BELLIED PARROTS (*P. rufiventris*) head, neck, wings and back rich brown, centre of chest and under colouring of wings bright red, lower chest and thighs green and yellow, rump green, overall length about 9 ins. with some variation between the sexes. RUPPELL'S PARROTS (*P. ruppellii*) head, neck and back smoky brown, wing butts and thighs deep yellow, rump greenish blue; charming little Parrots of about 8½ ins. overall length. From the island of Madagascar come the giant GREAT VASA PARROTS (*Coracopsis Vasa*), these are very large Parrots of about 20 ins. in length and are of a smokey brownish-black colouring throughout with the skin surrounding their eyes bare and whitish in colour. Their beaks are mostly horn coloured. The Great Vasas and their near relatives, the LESSER VASAS (*C. nigra*), are mostly kept in aviary collections as they have not really attractive features to recommend them as household pets, although individual birds have been known as great pals.

12. THE SOUTH AMERICAN SPECIES

From South America comes a very wide range of Parrot-like birds and for the sake of simplicity in this handbook they have been divided into the following groups: Macaws, Amazon Parrots, various South American Parrots, Caiques, Conures (macaw-like Parrakeets), Parrakeets and Parrotlets. Of this enormous number of Parrot-like birds the Amazon Parrots are by far the most popular and the majority of these Parrots make excellent talkers.

13. THE MACAWS

Macaws are a group of large, long-tail, bright-coloured birds with tremendously powerful beaks which can crack nuts such as Brazils with the greatest of ease. Their size ranges from about 13 ins. to 39 ins. according to their species. Individually-kept birds are as a general rule not very noisy, but when pairs or more than one species are kept together in a confined space they can create a very great deal of sound. Owing to their very powerful beaks they must always be housed with this thought in mind and also they must at all times be handled carefully. They are not as a rule very fluent talkers, but can be tamed to an amazing degree considering their size and powerful beaks.

14. HYACINTHINE MACAWS (*Aodorhyncus hyacinthinus*)

When in full plumage these Macaws are said to be the most handsome of all these wonderfully coloured birds; they are large in size being about 39 ins. in overall length of which about 24 ins. are taken up by their long tapering tails. Except for their dark beaks and yellow-tinted naked skin around their eyes they are a most beautiful deep hyacinth blue colouring throughout. Owners of these birds have always remarked how gentle and good natured they are, providing they are reasonably young when taken as pets into a household.

15. RED AND BLUE MACAWS (*Ara chloropters*)

These and those in the next two paragraphs are probably the best known and the most widely kept of all the Macaws. The Red and Blue Macaws are two or three inches smaller than the Hyacinthines and their plumage is attractively coloured in red, blue and green. Their bright colours and amusing antics always make them particularly attractive to children with whom they are invariably most gentle.

16. RED AND YELLOW MACAWS (*Ara Macao*) (Fig. 3)

Similar in size and general behaviour to the Red and Blue Macaws, their plumage colouring is red, yellow and blue in a most striking arrangement and their beaks are light horn coloured on top and dark underneath with the bare cheek patches pinkish white.

17. BLUE AND YELLOW MACAWS (*Ara ararauna*)

These   are   smaller   birds   than   the   two   previously

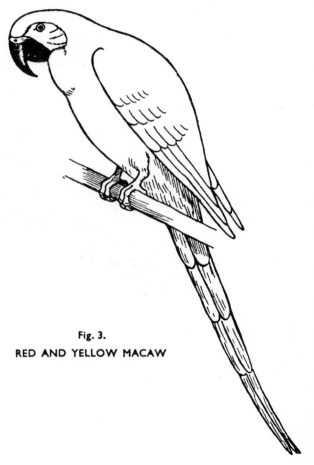

Fig. 3.

RED AND YELLOW MACAW

mentioned Macaws, being generally about 30 ins. to 32 ins. in
overall length; their main colours are blue on the upper parts of

their bodies and yellow on the underparts and the under surfaces of both wings and tail. Their beaks are dark coloured and very powerful. However, they can be quickly tamed if taken in hand when young, but their vocal powers of imitation are of a somewhat limited range although their natural voice is very powerful indeed.

18. MILITARY MACAWS (*Ara militaris*)

These are sometimes called the Giant Green Macaws because of the large amount of green colouring in their plumage; their beaks are dark, their heads red and blue, their flight feathers blue, rump and underparts of tail blue, upper parts of tail red and the remainder of the body colouring, various shades of green. They are said to be very easy to handle and make delightful pets.

19. OTHER MEMBERS OF THE MACAW SPECIES

The following Macaws are occasionally imported into this country and young birds of the different kinds mostly make good household pets. HAHNS' MACAWS (*Diopsittaca Hahni*) these are quite small for Macaws being only about 13 ins. long, their main colour is green on back and dull red on wing covets and underparts with a bluish tint on their foreheads. ILLIGERS MACAWS (*Ara Maracana*) smallish birds, about 16 ins. to 18 ins. in length mainly green in colour with red patches on underparts. These birds have been bred in captivity several times and the young reared successfully. SPIX'S MACAWS (*Cyanopsitta Spixii*) pleasing birds of a silvery, greyish-blue colouring which is set off to advantage by the dark naked skin patches surrounding their eyes.

20. THE AMAZON PARROTS

Next to the African Grey Parrots in popularity come the Amazon Parrots in their many different kinds. The Amazon Parrots have the largest number of different species in any one group. The prevailing colour of the Amazon is green ornamented in different ways with many shades of red, blue and yellow. The powers of imitation possessed by some of the species of the

Amazons is remarkable and as a general rule all the species are
hardy and easy to train. Some Amazons live to a great age and
their abilities as linguists rival those of the best African Greys.

21. BLUE-FRONTED AMAZONS (*Amazons aestive*) (Fig. 4)
These Parrots are about 15 ins. in overall length which is the
average size of the Amazon group. Like all of their species their
main colour is green with blue on their foreheads (which gives
them their name) running into yellow on top of their heads,
cheeks, throat and upper chest, wings edged with red. Blue-
fronts are imported in greater numbers than most of the Amazons and have much to recommend them as pets. They are
hardy, gentle with their owners, quick to learn and speak with a
clear tone.

22. YELLOW-FRONTED AMAZONS (*Amazons ochrocephala*)
These are very similar in size and in general behaviour to the
Blue-fronted which they press closely for popularity. They are
very like the Blue-fronted in their colour except that the blue
forehead is replaced by bright, clear yellow which fades into a
greenish shade at the back of head; edges of wings are red.

23. GOLDEN-NAPED AMAZONS (*Amazons auro-pallista*)
These are very delightful birds of an inch or so less in length
than the two aforementioned species. As their name indicates,
their outstanding feature is the deep yellow colouring on their
necks; their foreheads are yellow to yellowish green and the
edges of their wings and secondary flight feathers are red.

24. YELLOW-SHOULDERED AMAZONS (*Amazona ochroptera*)
These are not quite so frequently seen in this country as the
Golden-naped although their owners always speak most highly
of their good nature and their capacity for learning. Their main
colour is green edged with black, with top of head, face and
throat yellow fading into white on the forehead. The chest and
lower neck bluish with the wing butts yellow.

25. FESTIVE AMAZONS (*Amazona festiva*)
These birds are a little more colourful than most of their group

and make very attractive pets. They are of average size and their main colour is bright green with a dull band of red on forehead

Fig. 4.   BLUE-FRONTED AMAZON

and red on rump, with blue on cheeks, throat and streaks over the eyes.

26. SOME OTHER MEMBERS OF THE AMAZON GROUP

There are some forty other species of the Amazons, specimens of which are seen from time to time and it is not thought necessary to give the names and details of all of these birds. However, the following may be met with a little more frequently. LEVAILLANTS AMAZONS (*Amazona oratix*) head and neck yellowish-white with deeper colour on cheeks and light-coloured beaks, wing butts yellow and red, lower covets also red and the remainder of the plumage green. GUILDINGS AMAZON (*Amazona guilddingii*) one of the largest of the group being about 17 ins. in overall length. Head white; neck light green; back, underparts and wing covets rich light brown with wings of green, orange and blue. MEALY AMAZON (*Amazona farinosa*) head yellow; neck and upper parts mealy; edge of wings red, remainder of colouring green. ACTIVE AMAZON (*Amazona agilis*) these are one of the smallest members of the group being only about 10 ins. in overall length. Main colouring green with bluish tinting on top of head and red primary feathers.

27. VARIOUS OTHER SOUTH AMERICAN PARROTS

In addition to the large and interesting group of Amazon Parrots, a number of other Parrot species come from South America. The majority of these are quite brightly coloured and will learn to talk in varying degrees of fluency: they will all become quite tame if taken in hand when they are young birds.

28. VIOLET PARROTS (*Pionus fuscus*)

These Parrots are delightful little birds of just over 10 ins. in length; their tail, under tail covets and flights are violet; head dull, deep blue; back brown becoming pinkish at the edges of the feathers; chest greyish-purple. Violet Parrots make very nice quiet attractively-coloured pets and quickly become exceedingly tame and friendly. Their vocabulary is not usually extensive and the voice is small, but nevertheless clear. They are very friendly birds and similar in practically all respects to the Senegal Parrots.

29. RED-VENTED PARROTS (*Pionus menstruus*)

These are near relatives of the Violet Parrots which they resemble very closely in their general habits and behaviour. They are blue on head, neck and upper parts of breast; back and underparts greenish bronze; beak horn-coloured and ear patches black; the under tail covets vivid red splashed with green and blue. There are several other members of the Pionus group, but they are only seen on rare occasions in this country.

30. HAWK-HEADED PARROTS (*Deroptyus accipitrinus*)

These are quite striking-looking Parrots of about 14 ins. in total length. They are brown striped with buff on the head which gives them their strange hawk-like appearance. Their chest colour is red, edged with blue and the nape and back of head feathers are blue tipped with red, with the remainder of the body green in colour. Owners of these birds say they become reasonably tame and take very kindly to captivity and will, with perseverance, imitate a few words.

31. GREEN-THIGHED CAIQUE (*Pionites leucogaster*)

These are smallish birds of about 9 ins. to 10 ins. in overall length with rather shrill voices for ordinary household pets, but nevertheless they can be taught to talk and become very tame and playful. Their main colouring is green with head and neck orange and cheeks tinted yellow; chest patch whitish. Although not very strikingly coloured, these birds can be seen to advantage in an aviary in preference to a cage.

32. YELLOW-THIGHED CAIQUE (*Pionites xanthomera*)

As above, only with yellow colouring on their thighs: they are similar in size, habits and behaviour to the Green-thighed. BLACK-HEADED CAIQUE (*P. melanocephala*) only occasionally imported. Head black; cheeks and collar deep yellow; back, neck and wings green; thighs, flanks and tail covets orange.

33. PARROTS OF THE MALAY STATES AREA

From the Malay Archipelago come several most interesting and beautifully coloured Parrots, foremost of which is the Eclectus group. In their wild state the Eclectus live partly on ripe sweet fruits, but they will thrive well on a mainly all-seed diet if they are initiated gradually to this method of feeding; they will, of course, need some fruit. They do not seem to have very great powers of mimicry and are rarely kept solely as pets although they will become exceedingly tame and most friendly with their owners.

34. GRAND ECLECTUS (*Lorius roratus*)

These are fine birds with the males being about 17 ins. in overall length and the females usually slightly less. The unusual thing about the birds of this group is that their feathers have a hair-like appearance in contrast with the smooth feathering of the majority of the Parrots. Also the main colours of the males are green and red whereas those of the females are red and blue, making the matter of sexing quite simple. The males are green with deep blue flights, under covets and large patches on their sides vivid red, the beak is red, tipped with yellow, which sets off their colouring to advantage. The females are crimson red on head, back, wings, rump and tail; nape of neck purple and chest purplish blue and the beak black. These birds do make most decorative house birds and are not at all noisy, but as mimicry is not their strong point they are seldom seen as pets. Other Eclectus Parrots include the RED-SIDED ECLECTUS (*L. Pectoralis*), CARDINAL ECLECTUS (*L. cardinalis*), and WESTERMAN'S ECLECTUS (*L. Westermanni*).

35. RACKET-TAIL PARROTS (*Prioniturus platurus*)

These are smallish Parrots of about 13 ins. overall length, which includes their somewhat strange tail feathering. Their main colouring is green; nape and mantle areas pink and lavender and the covets lilac. Their two central tail feathers are shaft-like with webbing at the ends only, giving them the appearance of two minute rackets, hence their name. These unusual birds are seldom imported, and being rather costly are found usually in the aviaries of large collectors. Two other unusual Parrots from the same area are the GREAT BILLED PARROTS (*Tanygnathus megalorhyuckos*), brightly coloured with very large powerful red beaks, and PEQUETS PARROTS (*Psittrichas pecquetii*), large birds with bare black faces and black elongated beaks.

36. SHINING PARROTS (*Pyrrhulopsis splendens*)

These are very beautiful birds of about 18 ins. overall length and come from the Fiji Islands area. Their head, neck and underparts are resplendent in shining crimson red; nape of neck bright blue with the back and rump green. They live mainly on a seed diet, but they must always have a regular supply of fresh fruit and green food to keep them healthy and in full plumage.

37. HANGING PARROTS
These are quaint little Parrots of between 5¼ ins. and 6 ins. in length which spend a great deal of their time hanging upside down from their perches. They feed on fresh fruit and a soft food mixture. There are several members of the group the foremost being the BLUE-CROWNED HANGING PARROTS (*Coryllis galgulus*), their main colour is bright green with a patch of blue on the crown and a yellow patch on back and lower rump, with a red spot under the lower part of the beak. These little birds are not talkers and are invariably kept because of their unusual habits.

38. COCKATOOS
These are a rather wide group of fairly large birds which are inclined to be noisy when excited. As a general rule Cockatoos are great talkers, and even if they do not say as many different words and sentences as the Greys and Amazons they make up for it by repetition. Cockatoos are always attractive birds because of their colouring and their beautifully tinted crests which they can raise or lower at will. Taken collectively Cockatoos are most friendly both to other birds and to human beings and are very amenable to being trained. They have a reputation for living to a great age and are very easy to feed and manage and seem equally at home in cages, on stands, or in aviaries.

39. GREAT SULPHUR-CRESTED COCKATOOS (*Kakatoe galerita*)
There are several kinds of the Sulphur-crested Cockatoos or Lemon-crested as they are also called, which are more or less commonly known, ranging from the Great which are about 20 ins. in overall length to the Dwarf which are just over 12 ins. in length. The general colour of these birds is white and the crest and ear covets are sulphur yellow with the beak black. As a general rule these large Cockatoos are kept chained by a leg on parrot stands which allows the birds a certain amount of extra freedom of wing movement. The chains are very light, strong metal, and do not cause the birds any inconvenience. Like most of their kind they are very fond of bathing. Owners, of these and several of the larger Cockatoos mentioned in the following paragraphs, say how gentle these big birds are. They seldom attempt to bite

even when provoked. The author knows of a Great Sulphur-crested who has as his constant companion a little Blue Budgerigar and will not settle down for the night until he has seen his little friend's cage placed close by his side. It is quite common for large Parrot-like birds to form strong attachments with quite small birds of a different group.

40. GREAT WHITE-CRESTED COCKATOOS (*Kakatoe alba*)

These are another species of fine large birds of about 18 ins. overall length and are entirely white throughout including the crest, with the exception of the naked skin surrounding the eyes which is blue tinted, and a black beak. The dark colouring of eye and beak area gives these birds a far more attractive appearance than it would if they were all plain white. Many of these birds make excellent talkers especially so if taken into training when young.

41. GREAT BLACK COCKATOOS (*Proboscigar aterrimus*)

These are the largest of all the Cockatoos being about 30 ins. in overall length. They have very large crests, particularly when raised, and their beaks are long and extremely powerful. Their colouring is a uniform black with a greenish gloss throughout, although generally speaking the colour appears to be on the greyish side owing to a natural white dust which comes from the base of the feathers and skin. All Parrot-like birds have this peculiarity, but it only really shows up on birds with very dark or black plumage. The naked cheek areas are wrinkled and of a deep reddish colouring. They are only striking because of their size and unusual sombre colouring, but are not generally counted as being ideal pet birds. A few black Cockatoos have been known to talk reasonably well with a clear rather bell-like tone. There are several other black Cockatoos of which the BANKSIAN COCKATOOS (*Calyptorhynchus Banksii*) are the best known and probably the most widely kept. They are more colourful and not so large as the Great. Their colouring is mainly glossy greenish black with a wide crimson band on tail with the cheeks and neck speckled with yellow, this yellow and red colouring on the black gives these Cockatoos a rather pleasing appearance.

Fig. 5.
LEADBEATERS COCKATOO

42. LEADBEATERS COCKATOOS (*Kakatoe Leadbeateri*) (Fig. 5)

These are medium-sized birds of about 16 ins. overall length and their colouring is quite pleasing and gay. Their crest colour consists of bands of white, red, yellow and red which is seen to special advantage when fully erected. The rest of their colouring is white heavily suffused with a fine soft rosy red giving a lovely effect. Leadbeaters make very delightful household pets as they are very amenable to training, quickly learning to talk and mimic and are not generally given to using their own natural rather shrill voices too freely. One particular bird, Bill by name, was great friends with a Cocker Spaniel dog, and the two of them spent many happy hours playing together in thè garden. On winter evenings Bill delighted in sitting with the dog by the fire playing with his ears—much to the Spaniel's enjoyment!

43. ROSEATE (OR ROSY-BREASTED) COCKATOOS (*Kakatoe roseicapilla*)

These are the most popular and certainly the most widely kept of all Cockatoos both in their homeland, Australia, where they are called Galahs, and numerous other countries. They are one of the smaller kind of Cockatoos being about 14 ins. in length and most delightfully coloured in white, rose pink and grey. The crest which is white suffused with pink mostly lies flat to the head, being raised when the birds are pleased, startled or annoyed. The neck, chest and underparts are a lovely shade of rose red and the upper parts, wings and tail are of a soft grey, the tail being slightly darker than the rest of the body. Roseate Cockatoos are friendly little birds and quickly become tame and very attached to their owners. Their talking ability is somewhat limited, but the voice is clear and sharp. Although their beaks are small for Cockatoos they can nevertheless do quite a lot of damage if given the opportunity, many of them seem to have a great liking for digging out the putty from window frames. However, taken all round, Roseates are excellent birds for domestic pets, and another point in their favour is, given the right surroundings they will breed in aviaries in this country.

44. OTHER COCKATOOS

There are a number of other varieties of Cockatoo which are occasionally to be found as pets or in collectors' aviaries, but the aforementioned ones are most frequently seen. One rather unusual group are the SLENDER-BILLED COCKATOOS (*Licmetes tenuirostris*) which have very long, narrow beaks from which they get their name. They are mainly white in colour with head, neck and breast feathers flecked at their base with bright red. Another type which are striking are the BLUE-EYED COCKATOOS (*Kakatoe opthalmica*), white-coloured birds with long drooping crests and naked patches of blue skin surrounding each eye.

45. CONURES

From South America come quite a large group of Parrakeets which are somewhat like Macaws in shape and ranging from about 7 ins. to 17 ins. in length. Conures mostly make good pets as they quickly become tame and friendly, but at times rather spoil themselves by their shrill noisy voices. Once acclimatized they are extremely hardy and will thrive well on canary seed, sunflower seed, a little rape seed and some fresh fruit.

46. ST. THOMAS CONURES (*Eupsittula pertinax*)

These are neat little birds of about 10 ins. in length and are one of the favourite Conures. The crown of the head is bluish-green with forehead, cheek, chin and middle of under parts orange, the remaining areas green. These Conures are equally at home as single pets as they are in pairs, although the antics of a pair are certainly most amusing to watch. Single birds will become very friendly and with patience can even be taught to say a few words.

Fig. 6. GOLDEN CONURE

47. CACTUS CONURES (*Aratinga cactorum*)

These are very similar in size and temperament to the St. Thomas Conures. The top parts of the body are green with the crown a dull slate; cheeks, throat and upper breast brown with the lower breast orange.

48. QUAKER CONURES (*Myiopsitta monacha*)

These are very hardy birds and will breed fairly freely in this country. Pairs have reproduced quite well at liberty in the grounds of Whipsnade Zoo and it is quite a pleasing sight to see these Parrakeets flying and calling on the wing in natural surroundings. There is an unusual feature with these Conures, they actually build a nest of sticks in which to lay their eggs whereas the usual practice of Parrot-like birds is to nest in holes in trees or very occasionally in holes in banks on the ground. Quakers are about 12 ins. in overall length with the main colouring a fairly deep green; cheeks, throat and chest grey with a scale-like appearance; yellowish green on underparts and flanks. They make very nice pets and they can be taught to do tricks and also to say a few words.

49. GOLDEN (OR SUN) CONURES (*Eupsittula solstitialis*) (Fig. 6)

These are really lovely birds of about the same size as the Quakers whom they resemble closely in general behaviour. They are mainly golden yellow in colour with wings and tail green and blue. The yellow colouring deepens with age and fully adult birds of several moults are a beautiful shade of golden orange. Golden Conures are most desirable birds both as single pets or as pairs in breeding aviaries. There are many other varieties of Conures that are seen in this country from time to time and some of them breed quite well if given the right conditions.

50. LOVEBIRDS (*Agapornis*) (Fig. 7)

True Lovebirds are small, short-tailed Parrots and are quite distinct from Budgerigars* (*Melopsittaucus undulatus*) which are often wrongly called 'Lovebirds'. Lovebirds vary in size from 5

* These popular and delightful little Parrakeets are dealt with very fully in a separate Foyles Handbook *Budgerigars*.

ins. to 6 ins. according to species and the majority of them breed quite well in this country and several types have produced mutations of Lutino (Red-eyed Yellow) and Blue. Taken generally, Lovebirds although small Parrots, do not mimic or talk and only one or two odd cases of talkers have been recorded. Although this is the case it does not mean to say that more Lovebirds could be taught to talk if they were persevered with when young. They will become extremely tame and friendly and breed quite well both in cages and aviaries. The most popular of the group seems to be the BLACK-CHEEKED LOVEBIRDS (*A. nigrigenis*) which are dark green above and light green below; cheeks black; top of head red-brown, with bib a beautiful deep pink; beak red. NYASA LOVEBIRDS (*A. kilianoe*) are also quite popular with breeders and look very smart with their green bodies, red-orange forehead, cheeks and throat. PEACH-FACED LOVEBIRDS (*A. roseicollis*) are a little larger in size than the Black-cheeks and make most desirable birds for the breeding aviary. Their main colouring is deep bright green with upper tail covets bright blue and face and crown a lovely shade of peach pink. There has been some cross-breeding between the above-mentioned species, and also with some of the other kinds, but breeders are now trying, and quite rightly so, to keep the individual species pure.

51. AUSTRALIAN PARRAKEETS
From Australia and the surrounding islands in that area comes a vast array of beautifully-coloured Parrakeets, quite a number of which will breed in this country and many can be taught to say a few words. As the list of species is so very long to deal with they cannot all be fully described in this handbook. A few types have been selected to show some of the beauties of these Parrakeets.

52. ROSELLA PARRAKEETS (*Platycercus splendidus*)
These are very handsome, popular and free-breeding birds with a lovely blend of colours and are about 14 ins. in length. Head, neck and chest rich scarlet which is set off by white cheek patches; back black and yellow; rump and tail covets yellowish green. The majority of Rosellas (there are several nearly related

species) are hardy and docile birds and make tame and colourful pets.

Fig. 7. MASKED LOVEBIRD AND PEACH-FACED LOVEBIRD

53. RED-RUMPED PARRAKEETS (*Platycercus hæmatonotus*) (Fig. 8)
These are probably the most widely kept of all the smaller Australian Parrakeets and they certainly have many good points to recommend them both as pets and breeding birds. They are about 12 ins. in length and are mostly gentle with other birds and their natural call is soft and musical. Head and face greenish-blue; breast yellowish-green fading to yellow on the underparts; back bluish-green and rump bright clear deep red. Red-rumps are excellent birds for any new Parrakeet breeder to start with as they are so easy and simple to manage. There is a Yellow mutation of the Red-rumps which although not quite so brightly coloured as the Normals are most interesting to breed. They are hardy little Parrakeets and will thrive well on a similar diet to Budgerigars to which a little sunflower and hemp seed has been added.

54. MANY-COLOURED PARRAKEETS (*Platycercus multicolor*)
These birds are similar in size and general tempera-

Fig. 8.

RED-RUMP PARRAKEET

ment to the Red-rumps with whom they will hybridise. Head
and cheeks greenish blue: forehead, shoulders and under-tail
covets yellow; nape red; thighs and under-parts orange. These
are extremely pretty birds and make a wonderful sight when
flying in an outdoor aviary.

55. COCKATIELS (*Leptolophus hollandicus*) (Fig. 9)
These charming birds are sometimes called Cockatoo Parra-
keets as on their heads they carry a permanently erected crest.
Although more sombre in colouring than is general with Austra-
lian Parrakeets, Cockatiels have a quiet attraction of their own.
They are hardy, friendly, free-breeding, have a musical voice and

will speak a few words quite clearly. Their general colouring is dove-grey; face, throat and cheeks yellowish; ear-covets orange

Fig. 9. COCKATIEL

red and crest grey with yellow base. Single birds will get very tame and can be allowed the freedom of the house and some are so good they can even be allowed the freedom of the garden! Cockatiels have been known to breed quite freely and happily in the same aviary as Budgerigars and small Foreign Finches and have not attempted to harm their small companions in any way. It is quite an amusing sight to see a cheeky little Budgerigar bossing a much larger Cockatiel about.

56. RING-NECKED PARRAKEETS (Fig. 10)

These are an interesting group of fairly large Parrakeets consisting of about a dozen different species of which the best known is the common Ring-neck. A great number of these birds have been brought to this country both by service and civilian personnel serving in the Indian area. They are probably the most

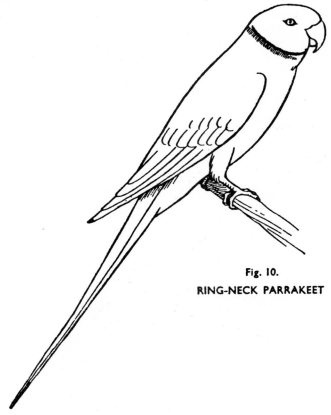

Fig. 10.
RING-NECK PARRAKEET

common of all the 'Polly Parrots'! All the species can be taught to talk and the extent of their vocabulary is governed by the particular talents of individual birds and their trainers. The two most commonly kept are the common Ring-necked Parrakeets (*Psittacula marillensis*); these are about 16 ins. in total length including their long narrow tails. Their main colouring is bright green with neck ornamented with a collar of rose-red which is bluish at the top edge; moustache and eye streak are black, and beak red. BLOSSOM-HEADED PARRAKEETS (*Psittacula cyanocephala*): these are slightly smaller than the common Ring-necked and are a little more sedate in their demeanour. They are charming birds of very gentle habits and are quite easy to train to talk. The head is coloured red in front which gradually fades to a lovely plum-bloom shade to the nape, below this is a black collar broadest at front; red patch on wings; green on back and greenish-yellow underparts.

Fig. II. SWAINSON'S LORIKEET

57. LORIES AND LORIKEETS (Fig. 11)

These are a group of beautifully highly-coloured birds varying in length from 8 ins. to 12 ins. and differing from the other species of Parrakeets in their feeding. These lovely birds feed on a diet of nectar and soft fruits both of which are abundant in the

Red and yellow Macaw

Colour photos by Colorbank

Pallid Caique

Black-cheeked Lovebird

Red Lory

Blue-fronted Amazon Parrot

Painted Concure

Ringneck Parrakeet

Mitred Concure

countries where they live. Lories and Lorikeets are not ideal birds for household pets because of their feeding, although numerous specimens become very tame and will even say a few words. In aviaries, however, they display their gorgeous colours to the fullest advantage and make a wonderful sight when flying. Below, two examples are described to give the readers an idea of the glorious colouring of these birds. SWAINSON'S LORIKEETS (*Trichoglossus Swainsonii*), these birds are about 12 ins. in over-all length with tail taking up just over a third of the total length. Head and throat blue; breast yellow and red; underparts red with dark blue patch in the centre; back, wings and tail mainly green with some yellow. Swainsons have been bred in this country both in indoor and outdoor aviaries and seem to make very good and attentive parents. RED LORIES (*Eos bornea*): these birds are slightly larger than the Swainson's which they resemble in many ways. They are practically all red in colour with wings marked with black and blue and the tail a dull golden red shade.

CHAPTER 3

HOUSING

58. THERE are numerous ways in which Parrot-like birds can be housed and kept successfully; each method will be dealt with separately in the following paragraphs. Individual birds and species can be spoiled if not suitably housed to the needs of their kind. A great deal of the success with talking pets depends on the correct and most comfortable accommodation. It should always be remembered that birds which are not comfortable and happy will never make good talkers.

59. CAGES

For pet Parrots of the African Grey and Amazon kinds, the conventional round or square all-wire cages are by far the most suitable type to use. The actual size of the cages varies according to the size of the bird which is to be housed. As a general rule the size for the big Amazon Parrots and the big Cockatoos should not be less then 20 ins. square at the base and 30 ins. to 36 ins. in height. For the Greys and ordinary-sized Amazons, etc., the base should be not less than 18 ins. square and 26 ins. to 30 ins. in height. For Ring-necks, Senegals, etc., the base should be not less than 16 ins. to 18 ins. square and the height 24 ins. to 26 ins. Lovebirds, Budgerigars and some of the smaller kinds of Parrakeets do very well in the large-sized all-wire cage because of the nature of their droppings. These cages are of the box type fitted with a sand draw on which absorbent paper is fixed. It will be realised that the cages for the large Parrots, Cockatoos and Parrakeets must be constructed of very heavy gauge wire because of the birds' powerful beaks. Fig. 12 gives the general layout of an all-wire square parrot cage. It is usual to have a large-mesh wire grill just above the removable sand tray to prevent escape when being cleaned and at the same time to allow the droppings to fall unhindered on to the sand tray. The perches are made of hardwood, preferably oak, and have metal caps at each end to prevent the birds from gnawing them away.

Fig. 12.

ALL-WIRE CAGE

The round wire cages are made on the same principle as the square, the only difference being their shape. It is essential that the doors of the cages are fitted with a clip for fastening that is guarded by a shield, so that the birds cannot open the cage from the inside. If this is not done it is surprising how quickly the birds will discover how to open the door and allow themselves liberty at the most inopportune times. Parrot cages are all fitted at the top with a ring for hanging, but generally speaking the birds prefer to have their cages standing solidly on a firm table. The reason for this would seem to be that the birds prefer to be nearer to their owners and also they are likely to get more attention at table level. Although Lovebirds, Budgerigars and small Parrakeets thrive very well in large, all-wire canary cages, quite a lot prefer to house their birds in oblong wood and wire box cages. These cages are usually 24 ins. long, 15 ins. high, 12 ins. deep, with the top, bottom, back and sides of wood and the front made of removable wire panel, see Fig. 13. All wood used for cage making should be good, well-seasoned hardwood, for it is surprising how even small birds will find a soft spot and gnaw their way to liberty. Although these box-type cages may not be so decorative as the all-wire ones they have the advantage of preventing all draughts from reaching the birds.

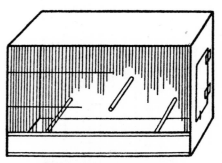

Fig. 13.   BOX TYPE CAGE

60. STANDS

Large birds like Macaws, large Cockatoos and Parrots are mostly trained to live on big 'T'-shaped stands complete with sand trays, see Fig. 14. These stands consist of an upright of tubular steel set in a heavy base and fixed to a round metal sand tray of the same diameter as the 'T' of the perch. This perch is usually made of well-seasoned oak, or similar hardwood, and at each end are fixed metal seed and water containers with removable porcelain linings. The birds are kept under control by a light steel chain which is clipped to the bird's leg at one end with a swivel clip, and the other is allowed to run free on a large ring which is fixed round the metal upright of the stand. These stands do certainly give the Macaws and the larger Parrots plenty of room for full wing exercise which would not be possible in an ordinary-sized wire parrot cage. As a change from their usual perch, birds often use the metal upright as a climbing post and

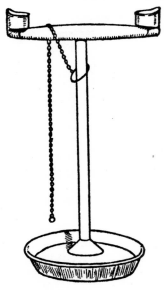

Fig. 14.   STAND

this they can do quite easily as the chain ring will slide up and down. The use of stands is the most convenient way of keeping large Parrot-like birds indoors. It must be stated here, provided the birds are trained to a stand, being chained by one leg in no way inconveniences them and they are perfectly happy and live to a great age in perfect condition with this kind of accommodation.

61.AVIARIES

Specially constructed aviaries whether indoor or outdoor are needed to house most of the large Parrots, Macaws, Cockatoos and larger Parrakeets because of the power of their beaks. Birds of the calibre of Macaws can cut through ordinary wire netting like a knife through butter and need heavy gauge metal bars to enclose them safety. Any woodwork used in the construction of these aviaries must be hard, strong and well seasoned and protected on the outside by metal sheeting. The best material for

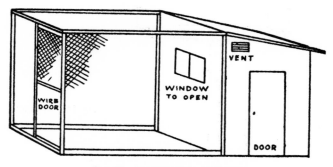

Fig. 15. STANDARD AVIARY

building the sleeping or shelter quarters is brick, as it is practically indestructible by the birds and the cost is quite reasonable. Small Parrots, Parrakeets, Lovebirds, etc., can be housed in Budgerigar-type aviaries if strongly built and wired with good quality wire netting, see Fig. 15. It may be necessary to double wire certain places in these aviaries and also to wire any woodwork that comes within reach of the beaks of the birds. The majority of perches should be made of hard wood so that they need not be renewed continuously. However, it is a good thing to have a few soft wood perches for the birds to gnaw and amuse themselves.

Aviaries are mostly used for the breeding of Parrot-like birds, and it is really surprising how many different kinds have already reared young successfully in captivity. Quite a number of species have also bred in large indoor pens; by this method many more breeding pairs can be housed in a given space. Water vessels used in pens and aviaries should be large and shallow to facilitate bathing which gives all Parrot-like birds great enjoyment. Some breeders give their birds small water vessels near their seed vessels and an entirely separate one for bathing in another part of their enclosure. This arrangement is a good one as it ensures the birds always having clean drinking water. The floor covering of aviaries varies according to their size; large ones having grassed flights and sanded concrete sleeping quarters and smaller ones all sanded concrete. Care must be taken to ensure that breeding and sleeping quarters are free from vermin. Although mice will not attack large birds they will very often disturb them whilst nesting, causing them to leave their eggs or even their young. A concreted floor together with small ($\frac{1}{2}$-in.) mesh wire netting 18 ins. up the sides of all the wooden structures, will make them safe against the larger vermin. Any mice which invade the enclosures can be exterminated by the careful placing of *covered* traps. The inside brick or woodwork of aviaries should be decorated with limewash or good quality distemper. However, if paint is used it should be of non-poisonous kind as many lead-base paints can be harmful to birds if eaten. Wire and metal work from which all loose pieces of galvanising have been brushed can be preserved by painting with one of the many good bituminous paints now obtainable from all high-class paint stores.

CHAPTER 4

FEEDING

62. CORRECT FEEDING

IT cannot be too strongly emphasized that the correct food for the many and varied Parrot-like birds plays an all-important part in their being maintained as fit and healthy birds. Birds in perfect condition are always a joy to behold and they are extremely *unlikely* to contract any kind of illness. There are many brands of quite good parrot foods on the market, but although they are good they are not really completely balanced foods for all the types of Parrot-like birds. In the following paragraphs various mixtures of seeds to suit the different taste of the different birds are given, all of which have been proved by many Parrot lovers and breeders.

63. MACAWS, COCKATOOS AND LARGE PARROTS

A good standard mixture for these birds when kept as household pets is $33\frac{1}{3}$ per cent of equal parts of hemp seed, buckwheat, dari, groundnuts and maize, $33\frac{1}{3}$ per cent mixed sunflower seeds and $33\frac{1}{3}$ per cent best large canary seed. This seed mixture should be given fresh every day, the quantity will vary with the different species, but the owners will soon get to know their pet's capacity. In addition to their seed mixtures, Parrots, etc., need fresh fruit, nuts and green food regularly in small quantities to balance their diet. Individual taste in fruit varies, some birds like apples, pears or oranges, others bananas, strawberries or plums, or perhaps figs or dates, but practically all kinds of Parrot-like birds will enjoy grapes, either white or black. It is preferable when giving fruit to offer the birds one or two small pieces at a time. Each piece of fruit should be about the size of a grape and the birds will pick it up with one foot and eat it up completely, without any waste. As a change, a few raisins or a small carrot can be given. There is no doubt that birds benefit if their diet is varied.

Green food can be offered in the form of pieces of cabbage heart, crisp lettuce or spinach leaves, or garden peas complete with pod, and here again the quantities given at one time should be limited. Although Parrots are not copious drinkers they should always have an accessible supply of clean water for drinking. It is very essential that the drinking water is *never* allowed to get stale or germ laden. Another very important thing for the health of the birds, and one that is so often overlooked, is grit. Parrots are no exception from other kinds of birds and they need grit to assist them to masticate and assimilate their food. A small vessel of good Parrot grit should always be at the birds' disposal whether it is in the house or an outside aviary. Parrot grit can be bought from any first-class cagebird stores, in various grades for the different sizes of birds. Parrots also need a certain amount of lime for their general well-being and particularly so at moulting times. Lime can be given to the birds in the convenient form of cuttle-fish bone which is comprised practically of all pure lime. Most of the large Parrot-like birds will appreciate a few nuts occasionally, all kinds can be given, but the favourite ones seem to be walnuts and brazil nuts. Macaws are particularly partial to brazils which they can crack with the greatest of ease with their powerful beaks. Such foods as cakes, sugar, puddings, meat, fats, bones, etc., should not be given as they will often cause the birds to develop bad digestions and habits and are quite unnecessary for the birds' well-being. Also it is not wise to feed pet birds at meal times, because if this is done they will generally make a nuisance of themselves by clamouring to be fed every time they see a meal in preparation.

64. SMALLER PARROTS, CONURES AND LARGE PARRAKEETS

A good standard seed mixture for these birds when kept as household pets is 25 per cent of equal parts of hemp seed, large white millet, buckwheat, dari, whole oats or groats, 25 per cent safflower seeds and mixed sunflowers seeds and 50 per cent best large canary seed. As with the larger parrots the seed mixture should be given fresh each day and the owners will soon get used to gauging the correct quantity for their individual birds. The same fruits and green foods as mentioned in the previous

paragraphs can be given with the addition of blackberries, rasp-
berries, cherries, dates, chickweed, green oats and seeding
grasses. Some Parrots are very fond of Indian millet sprays, and
these can be given as very special titbits or when any bird is a
little off-colour. Various kinds of nuts, raisins and currants can
be given occasionally as a change from fruit. Fresh drinking
water must be given daily and grit and cuttlefish bone should
always be accessible. The foods which should not be given are
the same as mentioned in paragraph 63.

65. SMALL PARROTS AND PARRAKEETS, LOVEBIRDS, ETC.

A good standard mixture for these birds when kept as pets is
25 per cent sunflower seeds, safflower seeds, hemp, whole oats or
groats, 25 per cent mixed millets and 50 per cent mixed canary
seeds. Fruit, green food, grit and cuttle-fish bone, together with
the general management are the same as indicated in paragraphs
63 and 64. Fresh, clean drinking water must always be given
daily. The ingredients of all the seed mixtures can of course be
varied to suit the demands of individual birds and species.

66. LORIES AND LORIKEETS

These birds are not really seed eaters, but they can often be
given beneficially a little parrot seed. Their main diet is soft ripe
fruit, a nectar mixture and a little insectivorous soft food. The
fruits they like best are bananas, grapes, dates, figs and ripe
pears. A standard nectar can be made up by mixing two tea-
spoonfuls of Nestles milk or some similar kind of condensed
milk, one teaspoonful of honey, half spoonful of Mellins food
with four or five tablespoonfuls of *boiling* water. The actual
amount of water which in all cases must be boiling can vary
according to the desired consistency of the liquid. It will often be
found that Lories, Lorikeets, etc., prefer a little fine good quality
biscuit meal added to their nectar. When buying birds of these
types it is always advisable to ascertain from their previous
owners what kind of nectar mixture they have been having. It is
of utmost importance for the health of the birds that the soft
food and fruit are given fresh daily, and twice daily if necessary,
and also that their feeding vessels are kept scrupulously clean.

Certain species will appreciate an occasional meal worm or two and also a little insectivorous food. There are several good brands of insectivorous food on the market and it is sold with complete directions for its preparation.

CHAPTER 5

ACCLIMATIZING

67. CHANGE OF HABITAT

As it will have been observed from the previous chapters, Parrot-like birds all come from countries where the climate is far warmer than ours here in Britain and therefore the birds must be acclimatized to this change of temperature. Acclimatizing means adjusting the birds' general condition to withstand lower and varying temperatures without ill-effects. When importations are allowed they invariably take place during the colder parts of our year and this necessitates that all species must be kept indoors in an even, warm temperature. Freshly imported birds must always be strictly isolated for some months from *all* other birds which may be kept on the premises. The first sign of sickness, however slight, must be watched for and should any bird, or birds, appear to be unwell, expert advice must be sought immediately. It is very important that sick Parrot-like birds should not be neglected. If ill birds are treated correctly right away they will invariably come through their sickness without any harm whatsoever. Some new arrivals may at first be affected with diarrhoea brought about by the drastic changes of climate and food, but this condition mostly clears up quickly with correct regular feeding and an even, warm temperature. A few drops of T.C.P. or some such germicide given in their drinking water and a little medicated charcoal sprinkled on their seed is said to be very good for the birds. There is on the market at the present time a preparation of the M. & B. group which is of great value for curing many kinds of internal ailments in all species of caged birds. When this preparation is used special care must be exercised in correctly following the directions of dosage and remembering that there is variation in the size of the birds. This M. & B. product can be obtained at all good-class chemists.

68. GENERAL MANAGEMENT

The following points should always be observed when dealing with newly-imported Parrot-like birds. The owner must make certain that all cages, stands, pens or aviaries are perfectly clean, warm, airy and dry, dampness being a great enemy to the health of newly-imported birds. It is essential for the well-being of the birds that cleanliness of housing, food and water vessels and the actual food and water, is strictly and carefully observed. Neglect in this practical procedure may quite easily cost the owner the new arrival and possibly other birds housed in the near vicinity. The birds should be persuaded to eat their standard seed mixtures as soon as possible and this should be done without making the change-over too drastic. Many of the Amazon group and the African Greys are fed on boiled maize when first captured or taken as young from their nest, and if this is the case they must be weaned with considerable care. Gentle handling of the cage or stand is important if the bird is to be eventually a real tame talking pet. Quite often many good birds are spoiled as talkers through being handled badly during the early part of their life in captivity. If the owner of a Parrot, particularly a newly-imported bird, has the misfortune to get bitten, the wound must be medically treated at once to avoid the possibility of it becoming septic. Any birds being acclimatized should be kept in a steady temperature of between 65 degrees and 75 degrees Fahrenheit; it greatly assists in the process if the temperature is always maintained at an even rate. It is sometimes said that birds receive benefit during winter months by the use of artificial sunray lamps. This would appear to be an excellent idea as new arrivals must undoubtedly feel the loss of their native sunshine. Freshly imported birds have also been accustomed to longer hours of daylight in which to feed and our short winter days can be usefully lengthened by artificial light. All kinds of foreign birds benefit by artificially lengthened daylight hours, as it enables them to eat extra food thereby maintaining their essential heat. It is surprising how much better the birds will thrive, develop and keep in good hard feather when they have long days during the winter months. The majority of Parrot-like birds really enjoy a bath and they should be encouraged to indulge in their fancy when practicable. With the larger kinds it is not always possible to provide suitable receptacles to serve as baths, but this difficulty can partially be overcome by the use of a spray; excellent bird sprays can be bought at all good bird accessory stores. All bathing should be done as early in the day as possible so as to allow the birds to get properly dry before nightfall.

CHAPTER 6

BREEDING

69. MACAWS AND COCKATOOS

THESE birds are not very often bred in this country, firstly because of the high cost of true acclimatized pairs and secondly because of the very large, strong and specially fitted enclosures they need in which to breed. In spite of these facts a number of different species have reared young in Britain from time to time and also Hybrid birds have been produced. Macaws and Cockatoos are very slow in maturing and coming into breeding condition (our climate may have something to do with the lengthening of this time), and it may take some years before a pair will settle down to serious domestic duties. Breeding quarters for these big and powerful birds must naturally be large and very strongly constructed. Specially designed nesting boxes (Fig. 16) or large pieces of rotting tree trunks must be provided for nesting sites. The eggs, which are white in colour and quite small for such birds, range from two to six in number according to species. The eggs are laid on alternate days although incubation actually commences from the appearance of the first egg and lasts from about twenty to twenty-five days. Consequently there is a difference in the ages of the young in each nest from two to twelve days. The young are fed for the first days of their lives entirely on pre-digested food, and as they get older they are fed direct from the crops of their parents. The difference in age lessens somewhat the strain on their parents, as by the time the last chick has hatched the first is on direct crop feeding. Both parents assist in feeding their chicks and the cock birds usually attend to the greater part of the hens' feeding whilst they are incubating. In some species the cock birds also take their daily turn at sitting on the eggs. The young of these large Parrot-like birds often leave their nests before they are fully feathered or can fly; once they are out of their nest they develop much more quickly and it is not long

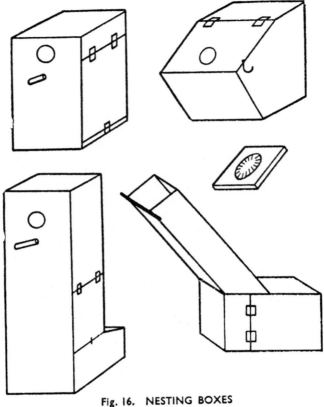

Fig. 16. NESTING BOXES

before they are feeding and flying quite freely with their parents.

70. AFRICAN GREYS AND AMAZONS

Members of the Grey and Amazon species are much smaller than the birds mentioned in paragraph 69 and consequently do not need quite such spacious breeding quarters. There are on record several instances where Greys and Amazons have actually reared young indoors, in large box-type cages. Any breeding aviaries or cages must be made of strong and durable materials, as these birds have very powerful beaks which the hens ply with great vigour when in breeding condition and looking for nesting sites. When young arrive the parents need extra fruit and nuts in addition to their standard seed mixture, also some good insectivorous soft food is taken by some species. When Parrots do start to lay, their nesting places must be left carefully alone as the majority of birds resent any form of intrusion upon their domestic privacy. A whole season's efforts can quite easily be spoiled by an owner being too anxious to look at the nesting site.

71. SMALLER PARROTS, CONURES, LARGE PARRAKEETS, ETC.

Many of these birds will breed in indoor or outdoor aviaries and some species such as Ringnecks and Australian Broadtails are quite prolific. Their general treatment is quite simple: clean, dry quarters with a suitable nesting log or box, plenty of seed, green food, grit, cuttle-fish bone, fruit and nuts, soft food and clean drinking water. Another very important point is that the birds must be left undisturbed as much as possible whilst breeding. Although they mature more quickly than the large Parrot-like birds, they nevertheless often take some years to come into the right condition for reproduction. Often birds are paired a year or two and live quite happily before they will even think about settling to rear a family. Would-be breeders should not be discouraged if their birds seem a long time getting down to business. The thrill of seeing the first young birds leave the nest will amply repay for the seemingly long wait for results.

72. SMALLER PARRAKEETS, LORIES AND LORIKEETS

A great many species of Australian and other Parrakeets are bred every year in Britain both in their pure and hybrid forms. A lot of breeders use Budgerigar type aviaries with extra strong wire netting allowing one pair of Parrakeets to each enclosure. Some species such as the Cockatiels and Redrumps have become thoroughly domesticated and with the latter a different colour variety, the Yellow Redrumps have been evolved. Many of these smaller Parrakeets have two broods of young per season, with the numbers varying from three to seven in each brood. Their general treatment is about the same as with the larger Parrakeets, but of course they do not require such spacious breeding quarters. Varieties such as Bourkes, Redrumps, Cockatiels, Rosellas, etc., have all been bred successfully in large indoor cages. Generally speaking, however, it is preferable to breed Parrakeets of all kinds in aviaries with plenty of flying space so the birds can have lots of health-giving exercise. Several species of the nectar-feeding Parrakeets—the Lories and Lorikeets also breed reasonably freely in this country both in large cages and in indoor and outdoor aviaries of varying sizes. The feeding of both adults and young is as indicated in paragraph 66. Many of these cage and aviary bred Parrakeets get very tame and quite a lot of them can be taught tricks and to say a few words.

73. LOVEBIRDS AND PARROTLETS

Taken as a whole the Lovebird family all breed freely in this country and many hundreds of young are produced each season both in pure and hybrid forms. The Parrotlets, although somewhat similar in size and temperament to the Lovebirds, do not take kindly to breeding in captivity, although individual pairs have occasionally condescended to produce families. The general treatment and management of Lovebirds and Parrotlets are very similar to that of the popular little Budgerigars and they like the same kind of seed mixtures with the addition of a little sunflower seed. Nest boxes for Lovebirds are of like design to those used for Budgerigars, but of larger dimensions, say, 9 ins. by 8 ins. by 11 ins. Lovebirds, although smallish birds, need quite large nesting boxes because they have an un-Parrot-like habit of lining their nests with bark, twigs and stiff grass or straw. At breeding times the pairs should be well supplied with nest-building materials, particularly in the form of green twigs from fruit, hazel, elm, etc., trees. Lovebirds are undoubtedly one of the best kinds of Parrot-like birds for the new breeder to start with to get a general idea of the management of the Parrot species as a whole.

74. GENERAL

It cannot be emphasized too strongly that with the breeding of any kind of Parrot-like birds, cosy housing, good correct feeding, absolute cleanliness and the unbounded patience on the part of the owner are most essential if any measure of success is to be achieved. The foregoing paragraphs have given readers a brief outline of the practical management needed for the breeding of the different species of Parrot-like birds and should help them to start in this fascinating section of aviculture.

CHAPTER 7

TALKING PETS

75. SELECTION OF THE BIRD

THERE are two courses open to the prospective owner of a pet Parrot-like bird—firstly, to buy either privately or from a reputed bird shop, a fully-trained talking bird; or alternatively to buy an untrained bird and do the training. The latter, of course, will be much less expensive. In the first case the bird should settle down in its new home within a few weeks and should commence talking freely according to its previous training. As a safeguard, however, a guarantee of the vocal ability should be obtained at the *time* of purchase unless of course the bird was known previously. With an untrained bird it may be some weeks or even months before it will even start to talk and therefore the new owner must not be discouraged if the bird does not begin talking at once. The previous Chapters have given readers information about the different varieties of Parrot-like birds and their varying powers of mimicry, and from them the choice of a pet can be made. It is always best to choose an immature bird for training as they are mostly more amenable to being taught than are older birds of fixed ways.

76. TRAINING RULES

A number of rules have to be followed carefully if the new pet bird is to become a talker. Perhaps the most important of all is that the complete confidence of the bird is gained at the earliest possible moment. Every endeavour should be made to prevent the new bird from being frightened either by animals or the sudden noisy appearance of human beings. If a bird does get badly frightened it may take weeks before its confidence is renewed again and in consequence its start in talking is often delayed. It is best if the bird is kept where it can see people moving about without being too close to them. At first one particular member of the household should tend to the bird's feeding and cleaning so that it gets quite used to the habits of one person. Each time the cage or stand is approached it should be done so steadily and without fuss and the particular word or words to be learned repeated in a clear sharp tone. It is a definite mistake to try and get a bird to learn too many words at one time and with most species it will confuse them so much that in the end they will only utter unintelligible noises. As a general rule all Parrot-like birds learn to talk more easily and more quickly if they receive their instructions from a lady.

77. VOCABULARY

It would appear from the observations of a great many Macaws, Cockatoos and Parrots that the sex of any of these birds make little or no difference to their ability to imitate the human voice. Many owners have great difficulty in ascertaining the actual sex of their pets and Tom, Dick or Harry, are often miscalled Mar, Jane or Sally! This, of course, does not have any bearing on their ability to talk. With smaller Parrakeets and particularly the little Budgerigars (which are true Parrakeets) the sex of the bird being trained has a definite influence on their vocabulary. It is only in odd cases that hen birds will learn to talk although they will become exceedingly tame and attached to their owners, making them most lovable pets. As indicated in the previous paragraph it is important to start teaching the bird clear, short-syllable words. The choice of a name for the bird is entirely in the hands of the owner, but whatever name is originally selected it should be adhered to throughout the bird's period of training. It is not necessary, as is a current belief, to cover up a bird when training it to talk, in fact, it is preferable for the bird to see its instructor and then to establish a really friendly relationship. However, if a bird is kept in the most lived-in room of a house it is quite a good plan to give it some form of shading from the direct glare of artificial light. Another belief which is quite *wrong* and very *harmful* is that the bird's tongue must be cut before it can talk. In addition to learning to mimic the human voice, and by the way they can learn any language, other sounds which occur in the bird's hearing will quite often be imitated. There are many

Parrot stories of which readers will no doubt have heard, showing the skill in which some birds learn to repeat the human voice. Other indications of the great popularity of Parrot-like birds are that they appear as characters in books, both for children and adults, and also songs and music have been written about them. During the course of the bird's training it is essential that the owner should always repeat the *same* word or words when approaching the pet and particularly when feeding or cleaning the cage or stand. It is only by continuous clear repetition that the bird will imitate its owner's voice.

78. TRAINING AND HANDLING

Because of the powerful beaks of many Parrot-like birds it will be realized that the vast majority of them cannot be handled with the same ease and safety as can most other species of caged birds, and that a special technique for dealing with them is required. Fortunately, however, Parrots, etc., do not require constant handling and, generally speaking, they only need to be handled for very special purposes such as sickness or movement to another residence. It is quite obvious that Parrot-like birds must be picked up in such a way that they cannot use their beaks to inflict dangerous bites. For the purpose of handling, both hands will have to be used and for safety's sake it is wise to wear light strong leather gloves. One method is to get the bird in a position so that a cloth or towel can be dropped completely over it, then taking hold of the bird in such a manner that it cannot bite. The other method is to grasp the bird quickly and firmly at the back of head and neck using a finger and thumb to hold the head in a safe position; this is done by putting them one each side of the head just below the base of the beak. Whilst one hand is dealing with the head, the other holds the body steady by grasping the bird just above the rump and including the long wing feathers. Some birds get very tame and will allow their owners to handle them with impunity and of course present no difficulty when they need attention. However tame a bird is known to be it is not wise for a stranger to put their hands too near the range of the bird's beak. It is a very good rule never to take liberties with any Parrot-like bird and vice versa. Every effort should be made to

prevent a bird being frightened or teased and this applies very
specially to the newly-acquired pet. A sudden fright will often
spoil the chances of a bird becoming a good talker. Teasing any
bird or animal is a very unpleasant habit and should always be
definitely discouraged.

79. BIRDS AT LIBERTY

Many species of Parrots, particularly some of the smaller
kinds, enjoy being allowed the liberty of the house and in some
cases can even be allowed that of the garden. When first let out
of its cage the bird must be carefully watched to see how it is
going to react to the privilege. The majority of birds are very
good when at liberty and thoroughly enjoy their spells of complete freedom. However, in a few odd cases some birds are rather
naughty and want to gnaw all and sundry woodwork in the room
that comes within reach of their beaks. Any bird that is known to
be of a destructive nature must only be let out of its cage when its
owner is at hand to keep it under control. Parrots at liberty
rarely fly; they much prefer to move from place to place with the
aid of their feet and beaks and it is surprising how quickly and
far they can move. Although Parrots can mostly take good care
of themselves against other domestic animals, nevertheless the
advent of stray cats and dogs should always be guarded against.
No doubt most readers have seen the amusing photographs
which appear in the national press from time to time of the
friendships between cats and dogs and Parrot-like birds. When
Parrots are allowed to go into the garden it is advisable to clip
the long flight feathers on one wing to prevent them from stray-
ing too far from home and getting lost. Parrots have strange and
amusing habits and the Author knows of an African Grey who
goes down almost every day to see its owner's chickens and gets
great fun out of sitting with them when they are laying; the hens
do not seem to resent Sam's presence and in fact they seem to
look forward to his visits. Another African Grey takes great
delight in climbing up the clothes post and then along the line
and pulling off the pegs holding clothes, much to his mistress's
displeasure!

CHAPTER 8

EXHIBITING

80. SHOWING

THE exhibiting of Parrot-like birds (excluding the Budgerigar) is only just starting to recover after the very serious set-backs of the war years and the period immediately following, to say nothing of the ban on importing Parrot-like birds. Most of these birds take kindly to being shown and a great many of them actually revel in the constant admiration they receive at all exhibitions. Birds such as Macaws, Cockatoos and the larger of the Parrots are usually confined to being exhibited at shows held in their immediate neighbourhood because the size of their cages presents transit difficulties, to say nothing of the high cost of freightage. With some of the more easily-bred Parrots and Parrakeets, exhibitions are a fine way of attracting new breeders of these birds and together with the non-breeding Parrot-like birds they always create a wonderful attraction to the general public.

81. PRIZE-WINNING QUALITIES

There is far more in exhibiting than just putting a bird in a show cage and sending it along to a show. Firstly, the bird's plumage must be complete and in perfect, clean, shining condition and the bird itself must be in good health and have no claws or toes missing. Secondly, the bird must be perfectly at home in a show cage or, with large birds, its usual cage or stand. Fig. 17 gives an idea for the show cages suitable for the smaller Parrots and Parrakeets either singly or in pairs. At the present time there is no prescribed show standard for individual species of Parrot-like birds because of their very great numbers, but there is a general standard of excellence which judges use as a guide.

82. TRAINING FOR EXHIBITION

Household pets require little or no special training for show work as they are invariably able to take such things in their stride. However, with aviary-kept Parrots and Parrakeets training is definitely necessary if the birds are to display themselves to their fullest advantage. It is so very disappointing both to the exhibitor and the public to see beautifully coloured birds hiding in a corner of a cage. As most shows are held during the winter months the question of interference with breeding operations does not fortunately arise. With aviary-bred and kept Parrakeets it is advisable to give some primary training when the birds are still quite young and this does save a lot of work at a later date. Generally speaking, however, Parrot-like birds take more kindly to being shown than many other species of birds and consequently require less vigorous training.

83. STOCK TRAINING CAGES

It will of course be realised that both show and training cages for Parrot-like birds will have to be constructed of very strong durable materials. The actual size of the training cages will be governed by the kind of bird or birds they are to accommodate. As a rough guide for birds up to, say, the size of Cockatiels (see Para. 55) the measurements would be length 4 ft. 6 ins., height 3 ft., and width 1 ft. 6 ins. For For large Ringnecks (see Para. 56) length 6 ft., height 4 ft., and width 2 ft. and so on in proportion. The floor of the training cage can be covered with a layer of good clean pine sawdust which will absorb surplus moisture and keep the birds' feathers in good clean condition. If Lories and Lorikeets are being caged then sawdust and blotting paper can be used and of course changed regularly, as there is always an excess of moisture with these breeds of birds. Seed, grit and water vessels should be put inside the training cages and the doors must be firmly secured as all Parrot-like birds have a knack of opening doors at the wrong time.

84. FEEDING SHOW BIRDS

The feeding of exhibition Parrot-like birds varies according to the individual species to which they belong, but it is fairly safe to assume that generally their standard feed plus the odd tit-bit is sufficient to maintain them in condition. One of the chief things to be avoided is over-fatness and on this issue very special care is needed with Parrakeets. When caged, the extra fattening seeds in the Parrakeets' mixtures should be reduced to a minimum. A regular and varied supply of green food should be given to all the different varieties. Fresh water, grit and cuttle-fish bone should always be available in the stock cages as these are all so very necessary for maintaining fitness.

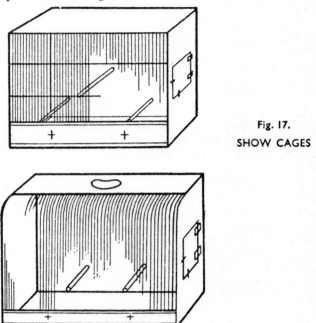

Fig. 17.
SHOW CAGES

85. SHOW CONDITION

The great importance of perfect show condition in all the many species of Parrot-like birds cannot be stressed too strongly, with show condition, good bodily vigour and perfect health must be combined with perfection of plumage. Show condition of the feathers means that the birds must have their full complement of feathers of good colour and texture without any being bent, frayed, broken or soiled in any way. It is rather difficult to provide bathing facilities for all the varied kinds of Parrot-like birds, but baths should be given wherever possible. However, spraying with a fine spray using clean, cold or tepid rain water or boiled tap water is a good substitute for baths and has a most desirable effect on the condition of the plumage. It is not wise to over-spray any kind of bird as it will make the feather texture 'ropey'. Spraying should only be done early in the day to allow the birds to dry out thoroughly and not at all when the weather is excessively damp.

86. SHOW PROCEDURE

When it is desired to enter birds for a show it is important that the rules which govern that particular show (show rules vary) and the section classification are first carefully studied. Classes for Parrot-like birds are mostly quite easy to follow and are usually limited in number, but should any doubt arise the Secretary of the show will always be pleased to advise. The entry fees together with the completed entry forms should be sent in to the Show Secretary well before the advertised closing date. Labels used on the outside of travelling cases (where the birds go by rail) must be fixed very firmly and the underpart of the labels filled in with the owner's name and address ready for the return journey. The inside cage card should be filled in with the cage number and the owner's name and address. When going by rail the fares must be paid for both forward and return journeys: British Rail will supply all details about sending live-stock by rail. It is important that before birds are packed for rail the water vessels in the show cages are emptied, many birds get their plumage soiled by this not being done. The train time-tables should be carefully checked to get the most suitable train so that the birds will arrive at their destination in plenty of time to have a rest before judging. When the birds arrive back from a show they should be put back into their training or stock cages and given seed and water and perhaps a special tit-bit by way of encouragement. It is advisable for any intending exhibitors to visit at least one exhibition before showing any of their own birds, so much valuable knowledge of show procedure can be gathered from a visit.

CHAPTER 9

AILMENTS

87. ASTHMA
THE condition called asthma seems to attack some pet Parrot-like birds that lack real first-rate health and are kept in over-heated, dry, airless quarters. When asthma first attacks the birds they get the typical wheezy breathing, but if treatment is given at once the condition is usually cleared up quite quickly. Birds that are affected should be kept in an even temperature and put on a very plain diet with plenty of fresh fruit, green food and water and then given one of the new effective asthma cures. These patent Avian asthma cures can be obtained at all good bird accessory stores.

88. BEAKS—OVERGROWN
The upper part of the beaks will sometimes grow too long if the birds are not given something to gnaw and wear away the surplus growth. Cuttle-fish bone, various nibbles and pieces of wood will all help to keep the beaks at their normal effective length. If the beak has become too long then the assistance of a vet. or an experienced fancier will be necessary to perform the operation. It is not advisable for anyone to attempt to trim a Parrot's beak on their own—who would care to, anyway!

89. BROKEN LIMBS
It is not very often that Parrot-like birds suffer from broken bones, but should an unfortunate accident occur the inexperienced owner is advised to obtain the help of an expert right away. Cleanly broken wings will, if left, usually set quite well on their own even if a little out of place. A broken leg mostly requires more detailed attention and this is best done by a vet. or an experienced bird breeder. A leg takes a longer time to heal than a wing and the owner is advised not to be too impatient.

90. BALDNESS, OR LOSS OF FEATHERS

Loss of feathers (other than natural moult) from various parts of the body is seen particularly in Parrot-like birds with the very aged and those having an ill-balanced diet. With the very old birds little can be done to ease the condition except by giving them foods rich in calcium and plenty of fruit and green food. With an ill-balanced diet the answer is quite simple: an experienced Fancier should be consulted and his advice on the correct feeding carefully followed. Any bare areas can be beneficially rubbed with fresh olive oil, having first cleaned the area with a good germicide. Repeated applications of olive oil will invariably help the feathers to start growing again.

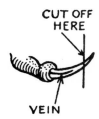

CUT OFF
HERE

VEIN

Fig. 18. CUTTING CLAWS

91. CLAWS—OVERGROWN

The claws of birds which are kept in confined spaces will mostly need their ends clipping from time to time to keep them from becoming too long and dangerous. Overgrown claws have caused many birds to lose their toes by becoming caught in the wire of the cage or aviary. It is essential that care is taken when the claws are cut and again it is necessary to have the assistance of a second person. See Fig. 18 for diagram of where the claws should be cut.

92. CONSTIPATION

Constipation will sometimes affect Parrot-like birds when their amount of exercise is very restricted and they are fed on a too rich dry diet. This dangerous state of health can be relieved and cured by adding a few crystals of Glauber or Epsom salts to the drinking water when needed. If the seed diet is a balanced one and fruit and green foods are given regularly throughout the year, constipation should not occur.

93. CONSUMPTION—GOING LIGHT

This wasting disease does not fortunately attack many birds these days, primarily because of the tremendous improvements in the conditions under which Parrot-like birds are imported and subsequently housed. Symptoms of consumption are loss of appetite, or insatiable appetite, listlessness and the steady loss of weight. If this disease is detected in its very early stages veterinary attention may be able to arrest and perhaps cure the condition. Sick birds must be put on a balanced diet, kept warm and given plenty of fresh air.

94. DIARRHOEA

Such things as fouled or stale foods, frosted or tainted green foods, will all cause diarrhoea in birds of all ages and of all varieties. If this distressing condition is allowed to develop and not treated at once the result may be most serious and perhaps lead to death. Birds so affected must be taken into a warm, even temperature and put on a diet of plain dry seed (made up mostly of large canary) and water (which has been boiled) to which a few drops of a good germicide or one of the new sulpha drugs has been added. Sometimes the feathers surrounding the vent area are soiled and evil smelling and if so need washing with warm disinfected water and dried with cotton wool. It is essential that the washed areas are most thoroughly dried to prevent the possibility of a further chill developing. If the treatment has been given in the early stages the condition mostly starts to clear within a few hours. Should no improvement be seen after about twenty-four hours then further expert advice should be sought. The sick bird's cage must be kept very clean and no other birds must be allowed to come into contact with the sick one, in order to prevent any spread.

95. EGG BINDING

Pet hen birds only get egg bound on very rare occasions, but in the breeding quarters it may happen through numerous causes such as soft-shelled eggs, damp or draughty quarters, over-fatness, under age or weakly stock birds, and the sudden changes in weather when the birds are about to lay. Egg binding is the inability of hens to pass an egg which is fully formed, through one of the causes mentioned above. Generally speaking, it is quite easy to detect egg-bound hens as they sit about on perch, floor or near the nesting box looking most dejected, with their feathers all fluffed out and breathing rather more heavily than usual. Should a sick bird be noticed it must at once be put in a cage and taken into a really warm room and the vent oiled with sweet or olive oil applied with a small hair brush. After an

Fig. 19. STEAMING EGG-BOUND HEN

hour or two of warmth the bird will generally pass the egg; in the more stubborn cases further measures may have to be taken. Should the oil and heat fail to give relief the next method is treatment by steam, see Fig. 19. Before putting the bird directly into it the steam should be tested with the back of the hand making certain it is not too hot. The vent and bare surrounding areas should be well oiled to prevent any damage to the skin. With the smaller Parrot-like birds, steaming is quite easy, but with the larger and more powerful birds assistance of a second person is needed. The steaming should be done for periods of about half a minute each and after three or four times in the steam the bird should be put back into its cage and the egg is usually passed within a short time. When the egg has been laid the bird must be treated as convalescent for several days and then gradually hardened off before it is returned to its original quarters.

96. ENTERITIS

There seem to be two kinds of enteritis—the contagious and the non-contagious, the former which is caused by a germ and the latter which is a kind of food poisoning. Both kinds of enteritis set up a serious inflamatory condition of the abdomen and if not treated quickly cannot be cured. The symptoms are diarrhoea, soiled vent feathers, swollen and inflamed abdomen and quickness of breath. The droppings of a sick bird are very loose, slimey, greenish-coloured and often tinged with blood and foul in smell. Treatment as with diarrhoea, paragraph 94. Inexperienced owners are advised to get help and advice in all cases of enteritis and even in suspected cases. It is always better to be safe than sorry!

97. FITS

Although some of the smaller and more excitable Parrot-like birds are subject to fits under certain conditions, on the whole fits are not a very frequent cause of trouble. Usually there is little that can be done by the owner, as the first indication of a fit is the bird falling from the perch with a flutter and dying as soon as it reaches the floor. Healthy conditions and correct feeding will make fits very improbable in all species.

98. PSITTACOSIS (*Parrot disease*)

Although this sickness is called Parrot disease it is in no way limited to Parrot-like birds and it can be contracted and transmitted by many kinds of birds including domestic poultry. One of the special dangers of Psittacosis is that it can be contracted by human beings and animals with most unpleasant results. The symptoms in Parrot-like birds are loss of appetite, fluffed-out feathers, watery mucus discharge from nose and mouth and severe diarrhoea. Any suspected cases should at *once* be put into quarantine and a vet. called in right away. All precautions, as with any contagious sickness, must be taken by the owner.

99. TUMOURS

Growths of all kinds are usually called tumours and they can be found on any part of the body. Although Parrot-like birds will live to a great age it is surprising how very few of them develop any kind of tumorous growths. In their first stages tumours do not seem to inconvenience the birds and consequently they are not noticed until they have a firm hold and are difficult to treat. Tumours on the upper parts of the body and wings can often be successfully removed by a vet., but when they are situated in the abdomen area they can rarely be treated with any lasting success.

100. WOUNDS

Sometimes Parrot-like birds get small wounds on various parts of their bodies which may bleed quite freely at the time, but very quickly heal if left on their own. Deep wounds caused by fighting may need stitching by a vet. so that they can heal cleanly and quickly. In all cases it is a good plan to dab any kind of wound with a good germicide and then dust with an antiseptic powder.

INDEX TO PARAGRAPHS